# CARVING CARICATURE NAMETAGS

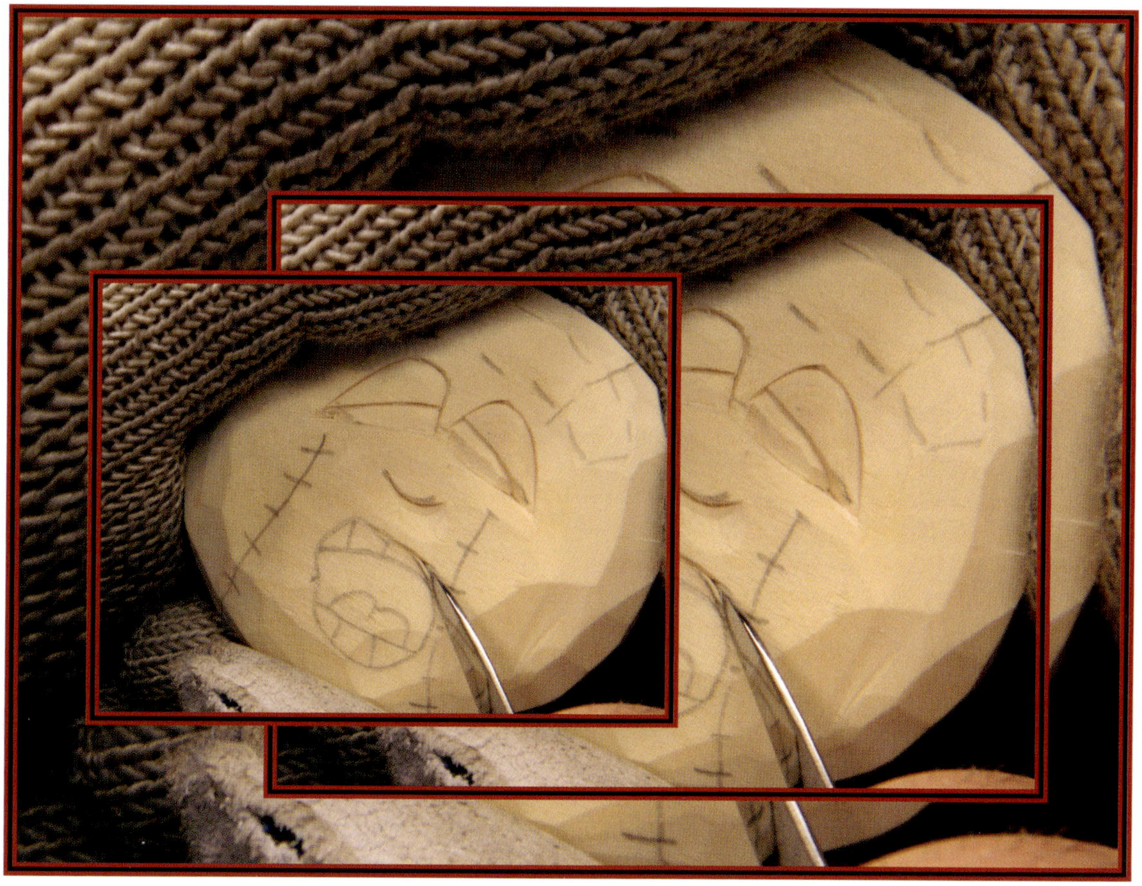

**CHRIS MORGAN**

Schiffer Publishing Ltd

4880 Lower Valley Road • Atglen, PA 19310

**Other Schiffer Books by the Author:**
Carving Caricature Bookmarks: A Beginner's Step-by-Step Guide, 978-0-7643-4083-3, $16.99

**Other Schiffer Books on Related Subjects:**
Carving Caricature Women, 0-7643-0-6499, $14.95
Carving Caricature Figures from Scratch, 0-7643-1233-2, $14.95


Library of Congress Control Number: 2013931112



Designed by RoS
Type set in Gill Sans MT Pro

ISBN: 978-0-7643-4187-8
Printed in China

Published by Schiffer Publishing, Ltd.
4880 Lower Valley Road
Atglen, PA 19310
Phone: (610) 593-1777; Fax: (610) 593-2002
E-mail: Info@schifferbooks.com

For our complete selection of fine books on this and related subjects, please visit our website at: **www.schifferbooks.com**. You may also write for a free catalog.

This book may be purchased from the publisher. Please try your bookstore first.

We are always looking for people to write books on new and related subjects. If you have an idea for a book, please contact us at: **proposals@schifferbooks.com**.

Schiffer Publishing's titles are available at special discounts for bulk purchases for sales promotions or premiums. Special editions, including personalized covers, corporate imprints, and excerpts can be created in large quantities for special needs. For more information, contact the publisher.

In Europe, Schiffer books are distributed by
Bushwood Books
6 Marksbury Ave.
Kew Gardens
Surrey TW9 4JF England
Phone: 44 (0) 20 8392 8585; Fax: 44 (0) 20 8392 9876
E-mail: info@bushwoodbooks.co.uk
Website: www.bushwoodbooks.co.uk

# DEDICATION

*I would like to thank my wife Amanda and daughter Avri, who support my carving, and to the many people that wear my nametags on a daily basis.*

# ACKNOWLEDGMENTS

*A special thank you to my wife Amanda for taking the photographs in this book.*

# CONTENTS

# INTRODUCTION

A few years ago when I was on my way back from vacation, I stopped at a theme park in Branson, Missouri. I had been there many times growing up and was always fascinated with the woodcarvers who were there demonstrating. In more recent years, I had always gone to the woodcarving shop and thought how nice it would be to start carving, but this time I had a little help with making the decision. My wife decided that she had heard enough of me talking about starting and took it upon herself to ask one of the carvers there to sell me what I needed to get going. The carver demonstrating that day sold me the items, gave me some blanks to practice with, and some pointers on knife safety. I took these items (and the information) the carver had given me back home and the next day started carving. I developed a passion for woodcarving since that day. I constantly practice, sketch new ideas, and talk to people who want to learn more about this art form.

Woodcarving has taught me a lot about myself and given me a great appreciation for the people who practice this art. Woodcarving can also expose you to lifelong friendships like the one that I have now with the carver who was demonstrating that day at the amusement park. I hope all of you who read this book develop skills that you can build on and keep you carving.

# 1

Sometime back I was asked to create a nametag for a friend of mine who sells baseball merchandise. He did not specify what he wanted...just something carved. So I sat down and sketched out this baseball for him. With this pattern, you can make the baseball as big or as small as you wish. I tried to keep it in the 2-1/2" size so that it was not too large and you could read the name. You can also play around with the expressions on these faces...adding more detail to them will really make them stand out.

## THE BASEBALL

The pattern we will be using for the baseball is a 2-1/2" diameter circle: cut the outline with a band saw or scroll saw.

Pattern is cut along the line...notice how the grain direction is running left to right.

I have marked the edge so you can see where we will be removing the saw marks.

Start removing the edge marks with a pare cut. You may need to change the direction of your cuts according to the grain direction.

All of the edge is removed; now start rounding the top of the pattern.

Start off by rounding off the top corner of the block.

Work around the entire block, on the outside corner.

Now start rounding from the top down towards the outside edge we just cut.

Your block should look close to this thickness on the end.

One side done...you can see the difference of the corners.

Three-quarters of the block rounded off.

The whole block is rounded down along the edges. Now we will work on the middle section of the block.

You will want to cut from the middle of the block towards the outside edge. Make these same cuts over the entire top surface of the block.

Round off any sharp corners to give the appearance of a round surface.

You now have a rounded block.

Your block should look close to this from the side.

Now draw the pattern on the block. Transfer the entire pattern on the block.

Our first cut will be a stop line along the top eye line.

Continue the stop cut along the line.

The first eye line stop cut at its end.

Now cut back towards the stop cut to remove the thin piece of wood.

The piece of wood has been removed and the side of the upper eyelid has been made.

The stop cut is made for the other side of the eye starting from the top, cutting down to the bottom corner of the eye.

Cut back towards the stop cut.

Left side cuts made along the eye. Continue the same process for the bottom line of the eye.

Bottom of the eye cuts are made.

Make a stop cut along the top of the eyeball from left to right and then make a cut back towards this stop cut, removing the wood.

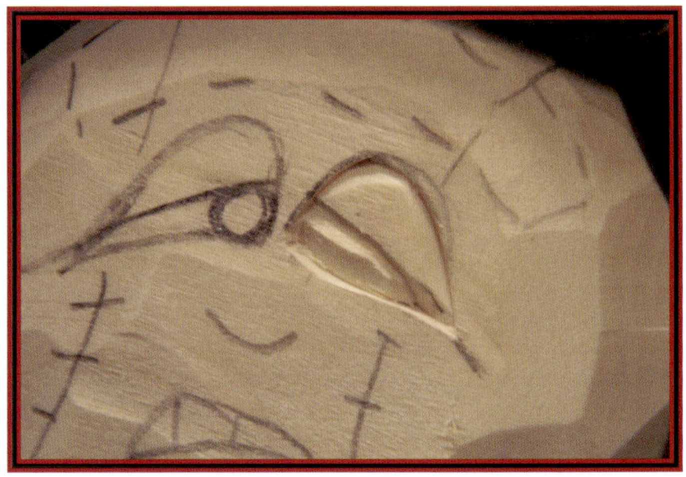

With this cut completed, the eyeball is now defined. Repeat these cuts for the other eye.

Both eyes are now completed; now it's time to work on the nose.

For this area of the nose, you will be making a stop cut along the line. This cut will not be very deep.

Cut straight down following the line.

With the stop cut made, you will be cutting back towards the stop cut.

Start by placing the point of the knife at the beginning of the stop cut. This cut will be fairly thin to match the depth of our stop cut.

Notice that the blade is fairly shallow as you start this cut from left to right. Cut to the middle of the nose as the grain changes.

From the right side, cut back towards the middle, removing the wood.

With the nose done, clean up any fuzzies that may be left behind.

The mouth area comes next: you will be making a stop cut along the line marked.

Make a straight cut down along the mouth line; this cut should be fairly deep.

Continue the cut all the way around the line of the mouth.

Repeating the same cuts as done for the nose, cut back towards the stop cut.

This is what the top portion of the mouth should look like. Repeat the same cuts along the bottom of the mouth.

Bottom mouth cuts made.

I marked the teeth back on the carving. You can draw these back on straight or at the angle shown.

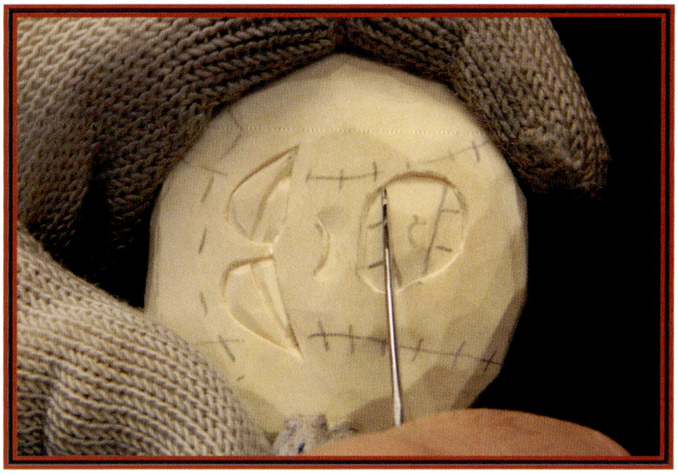

Make a stop cut along the teeth lines as marked.

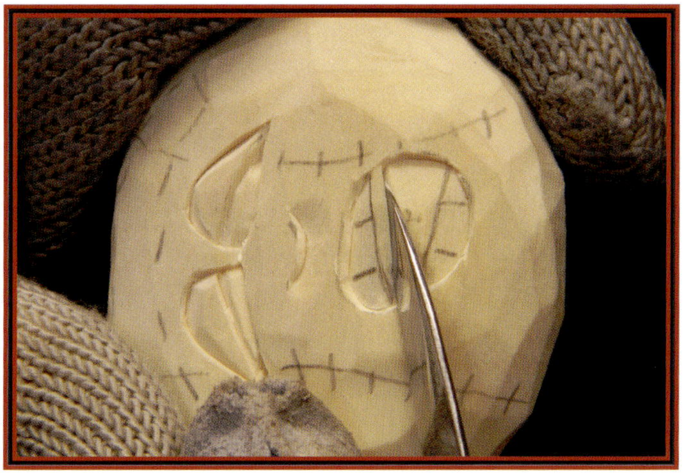

Cut towards the stop cut…this will make the teeth stand out.

Here is what the teeth should look like after completing the two cuts. Repeat the same steps to finish the bottom teeth.

We now have the top and bottom teeth completed.

Now cut the individual teeth marks. With the knife at an angle, make a cut towards the center line.

From the other side of the line, cut back towards the middle. These two cuts should make a "V" shape cut.

With one tooth done, I will make the same cuts for the remaining lines marked for the teeth.

Now I have marked out the tongue area. You can make this any shape you like.

Start by making a stop cut straight down along the tongue line marked. Once this has been completed, cut back towards the stop cut removing the wood in between the teeth and the tongue.

I have removed the material just enough for the tongue to stand out from the teeth.

Clean up the area around the tongue, removing the wood to the depth you are looking for.

Now mark the stitches on the carving.

With the "V" tool, follow the line working from the bottom towards the eye area. Do not cut the stitching line in the area designated for the name.

One side cut with the "V" tool. Notice that the stitches were not cut very deep.

Cut the other side the same way.

With both sides completed, cut the cross stitching.

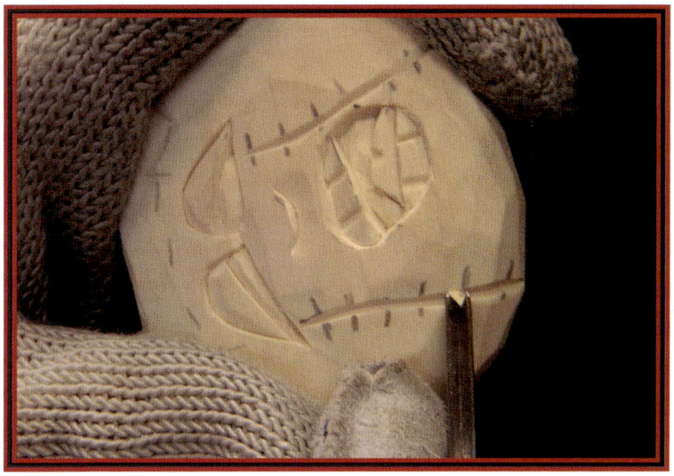

With the "V" tool, cut from the outside towards the center stitch cut. Cut both sides marked.

One side is complete. Repeat the cuts for the remaining lines marked.

Here I have completed the stitches and have penciled in the name in our designated area. I will use a wood-burner to finish the name. If you do not have a wood-burner, a permanent marker will work also.

I have the name burned and the carving part is done. All that is left to do is place the pin on the back of the carving.

Mark off a visual placement on the back, close to the top center. Keep in mind that different nametags will require different placements.

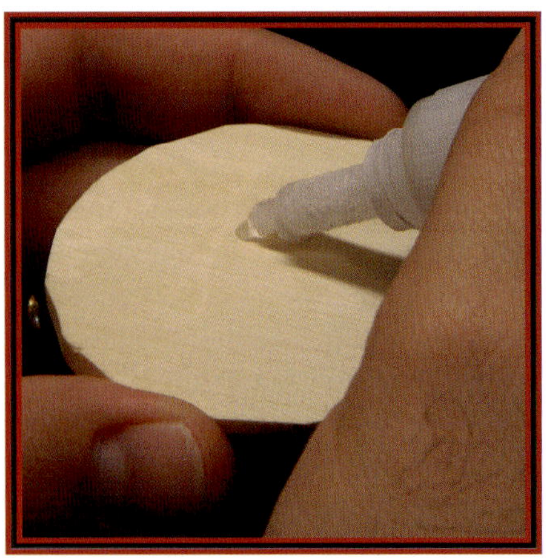

I use super glue to attach the pin's back to the carving. Make sure that the glue covers the entire pin back.

Press the pin back firmly into the glue and let dry.

Here is the painted baseball ready for its new owner. I used acrylic paints to finish this carving, but you can use any style of paints that you like.

# 2

This pattern is included in the Patterns chapter of the book, but it does not have the caricature face drawn on it. I took the plain pumpkin and added the caricature features to make it more interesting to carve. Most of the patterns in this book can be modified by giving them your own spin.

## THE PUMPKIN

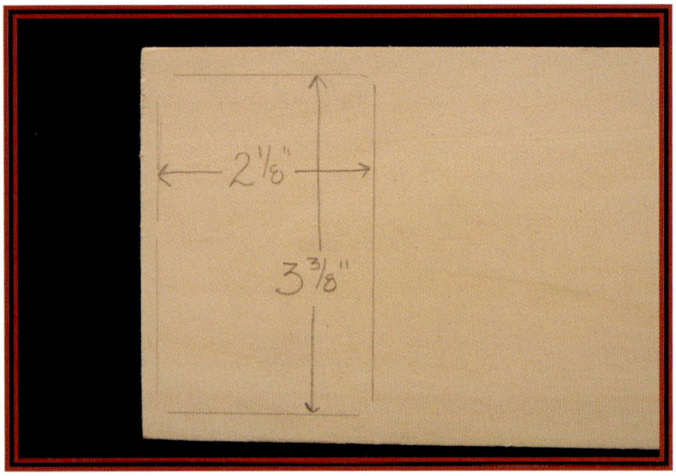


Our blank size is 2-1/8" wide by 3-3/8" tall with the grain running left to right. Cut the line marked with a band saw or scroll saw.

I have drawn the pattern on the block of wood and marked the areas that can be carved or cut with a saw. I will cut the pattern again with the band saw to get my starting shape.

Here is our starting shape — we are ready to start carving the pumpkin.

I have marked the grain direction. This project will have several cuts across the grain.

Begin by removing the band saw marks on the edges of the blank. When you cut on the outside, pay close attention to how the knife may want to dig into the block. If this happens, change the direction of cut to go with the grain of the wood.

Half of the band saw marks have been removed. Continue this process around the remaining edge.

Now block out the stem of the pumpkin.

Start by making a cut in the center of the stem, cutting towards the line drawn.

Now cut from the top down towards the previous cut, removing the triangle piece of wood.

Here are the two cuts completed.

Make the same cuts for the opposite side.

Both sides of the stem are done.

I have marked the top and bottom of the pumpkin with the next cuts we will be making. These will give us our desired shape and look we want.

Start by making a cut — this will be the first half of a "V" shape.

Now cut back to the first cut, creating the "V" shape.

We will need to widen the cut back towards the center …

… Just a little more cutting towards the center.

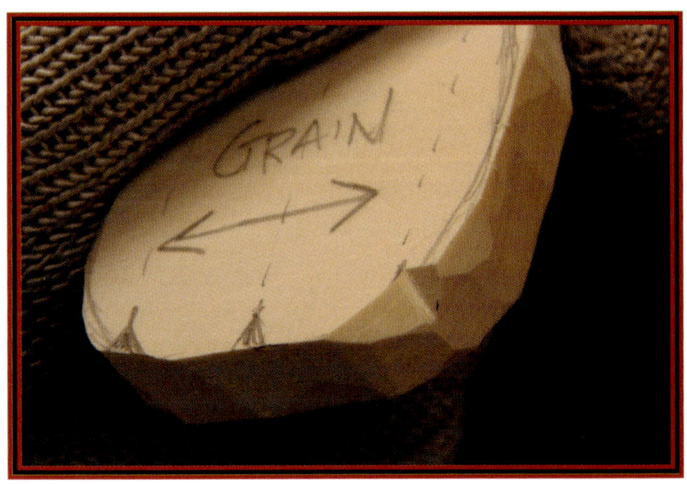


One end is complete. Continue the same cuts for the remaining areas marked.

The bottom notches are completed.

Now from the outside of the pumpkin, cut towards the notch, rounding off the corner.

This will widen the outside, completing the shape.

This is what the bottom corner should look close to.

Make the first cut at the top of the pumpkin to define the lines marked. Cut from the bottom towards the line.

Cut from the top towards the last cut we made.

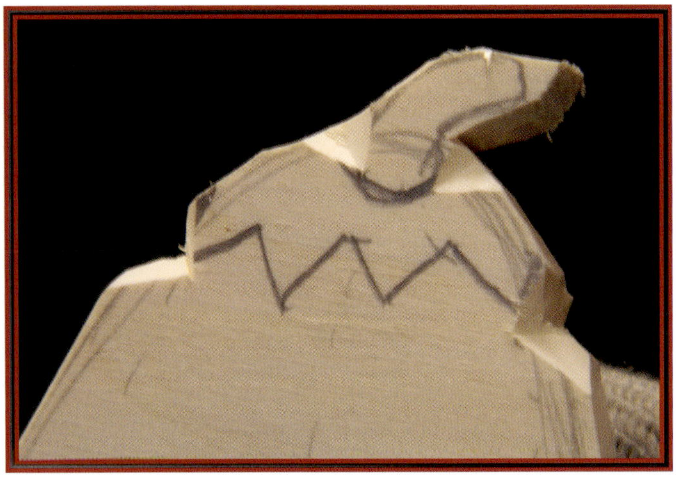

This will remove the "V" shaped piece. Repeat those cuts for the other side of the pumpkin.

This marked line will be our next cut. I will use a small "V" tool to make these cuts.

From the bottom, cut towards the peak of the lines.

Cut from the other bottom line back towards the first peak. Repeat this for the remaining lines.

Here are the completed cuts made by the "V" tool for the top of the pumpkin.

Now we will round off the sides... Cut from the top down, removing the edge from the block.

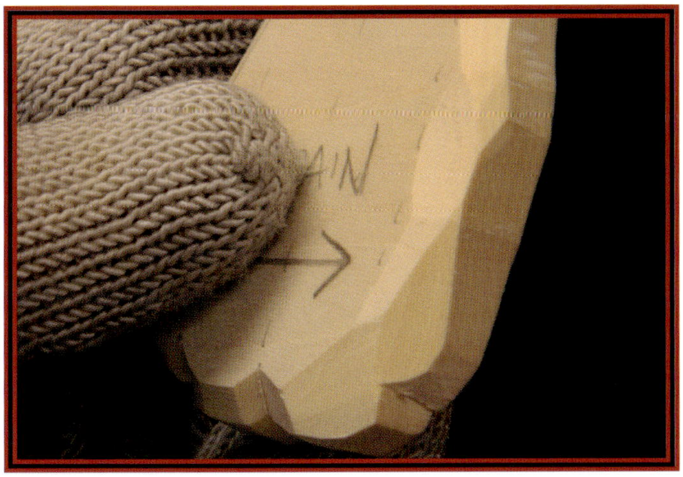

After you have made these cuts, continue to shape the edge. You can round this corner as much as you like to get the desired shape.

You will round the entire block something close to what is shown here. Continue to round the piece across the top to remove and flatten areas.

Your piece should look like this.

Now clean up the top portion of the pumpkin, removing any fuzzies from the previous cuts.

Clean up is done.

Here I have marked the eyes and nose for the next set of cuts.

Start by making a stop cut along the line from the top to the bottom.

From the opposite side, cut from the top down to the top of the eyeball.

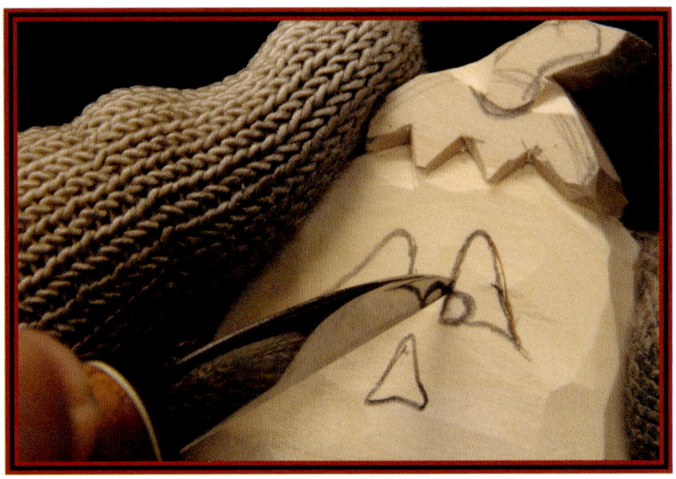

Stop the cut at the top of the eyeball.

From left to right, make your cut to remove the wood.

Continue cutting from the inside towards the outside line, removing the small amount of wood.

This is what the right eye should look like.

Now cut around the eyeball, starting at the top.

Finish the cut at the right corner of the eye.

Cut towards the corner of the eye to remove the wood.

The eyeball is now exposed. Repeat the same steps for the left eye.

Next, make a cut along the line of the nose, cutting from the top down.

Stop at the bottom corner.

Make the same cut for the left side.

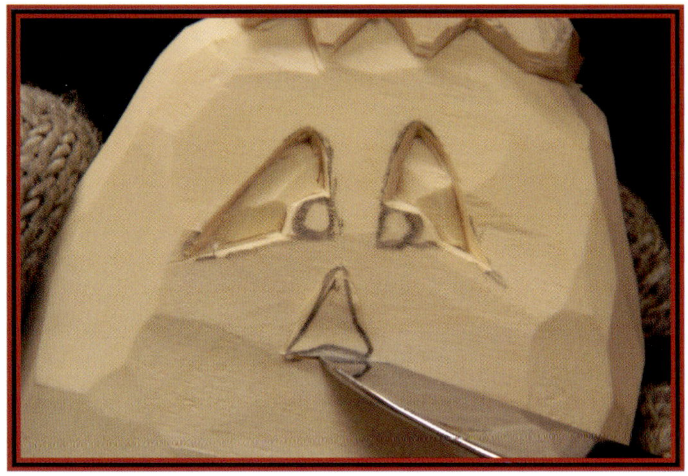

Cut the bottom line from left to right and the triangle piece of wood will come out.

The nose is done… Notice the triangle shape we created.

Now mark the mouth area.

Be sure the mouth is as you want it since we will now be cutting along the marked line, outlining the mouth area.

From the middle of the mouth, use the "V" tool to start cutting towards the left corner.

The cut is made... Now cut from the middle to the top right.

The top of the mouth is done. Continue making the cut with the "V" tool around the sides and bottom of the mouth.

The mouth as outlined with the "V" tool.

Mark the top and bottom teeth and write in the name. Use the "V" tool to cut along the teeth lines and the bottom vertical lines of the teeth.

Top and bottom teeth lines are cut.

Mark the vertical lines of the pumpkin. We will use a "V" tool to cut these lines.

Cut along the marked lines to define the pumpkins ribs… These cuts should be fairly shallow.

The "V" tool cuts are made.

The top of the stem area needs some finishing work. We will notch this area out to create a separated look.

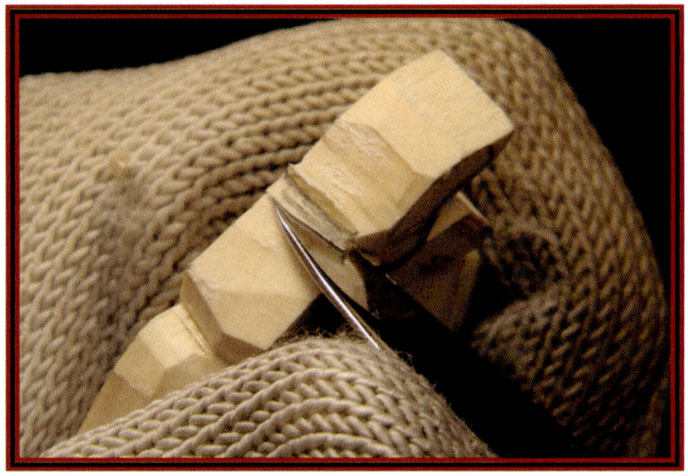

Make this cut towards the center of the stem and then cut from the top down, removing the small piece of wood.

Move to the front of the stem and make a thin cut starting at the bottom.

Continue the cut along the front, removing a thin amount of material. Basically I do this to remove pencil lines and reduce the thickness of the stem.

For the bottom of the stem, make a stop cut along the line starting on the left side.

Continue this stop cut along the line.

The top cut towards the bottom stop cut has been made. Remove the wood and clean up any pieces remaining.

The stem is cleaned up and shaped.

Now round the corners of the top under the stem on both sides, removing all pencil marks.

Just a little more thinning of the stem. This may be optional, as you may not need to cut any more if it looks good to you.

Here is the completed stem and top section. Clean up any cuts that may have been missed and remove any pencil marks remaining.

I wood-burned the eyes and name. Again, a permanent marker will work if you don't have a wood-burner.

Mark the position of the pin on the back of the carving. Place it close to the top center of the nametag.

Apply a bead of super glue or epoxy to attach the pin.

Press the pin firmly in place and let dry.

There you have it… A completed pumpkin nametag.

3

A very good friend of mine had carved this pattern originally for a lady who sold pottery. He colored the coffee cup a red, white, and blue theme and it turned out really nice. I thought that this pattern would make a nice addition to the nametag carvings, so let's have fun with it.

# THE COFFEE MUG

For the coffee mug, we want to mark the block with the grain running up and down. Cut the line marked with a band saw or scroll saw.

Here, I have marked the mug pattern on the block and the areas that we will cut away, as well as the hole to be drilled for the handle.

The pattern has been cut ready to carve. The hole should be just big enough to leave some material for the handle not to break.

I have also marked the edge where we will be removing the bandsaw marks.

Make thin cuts on the edge to clean it up. The grain will change in about the middle point of the block, so you may need to change the directions of your cuts to avoid splitting the wood.

One edge cleaned up... Continue cutting the edges along the rest of the block.

The top of the handle will need to be cut with the grain to avoid tearing the wood.

Cut towards the top of the handle to clean up the top handle area.

The edge of the mug and handle will be cut next.

Make a stop cut along the handle line from top to bottom.

Cut back towards the stop cut to remove a small piece of wood.

This is the result from the two cuts we made.

Now round off the edges of the handle and deepen the cut where the handle meets the body of the mug.

This is the depth we are looking for at the base of the handle.

Mark the inside area of the handle to round them off and thin them down.

From the middle of the handle, cut towards the body of the mug.

This is what it should look like...

Repeat these steps: cut to the top of the handle area and clean up the edges.

Now round the handle some more; take the material down to your desired thickness.

Rounding off the corners of the handle...

Continue shaping the corners of the handle.

Round off the bottom corners.

Here is our finished handle...

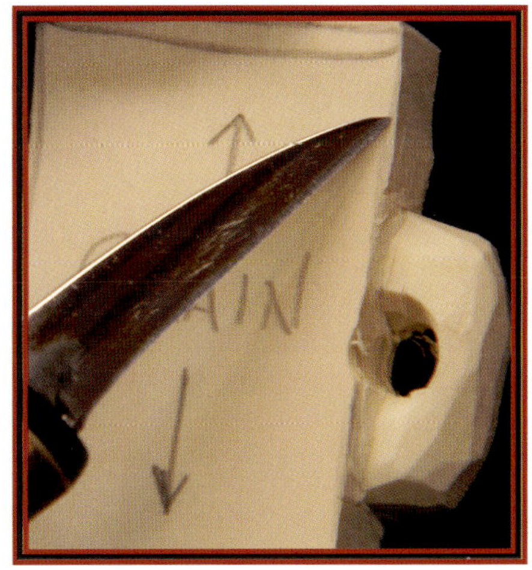

Now round the edges of the mug.

Start from the middle and work down the edge and then from the middle working towards the top. The grain changes in the middle of this block.

Continue making these cuts, working towards the center. This will give the mug a round appearance.

Here is the right edge completed.

Now round off the bottom of the mug.

With the bottom rounded and the corner gone, continue making the cuts until the entire bottom is completed.

Next, start working on the left side. Make the same cuts as we did on the right side, thinning down the block.

Work from the middle down towards the bottom.

Three sides are completed.

Now let's work on rounding the top of the mug.

We'll begin by removing a small amount of wood, each time starting the cut closer to the center as we cut towards the top.

The top is done — and now it's starting to look like a coffee mug.

With the middle part remaining to carve, our next cuts will be removing any flat areas.

Cut from the middle towards the top and then from the middle down towards the bottom.

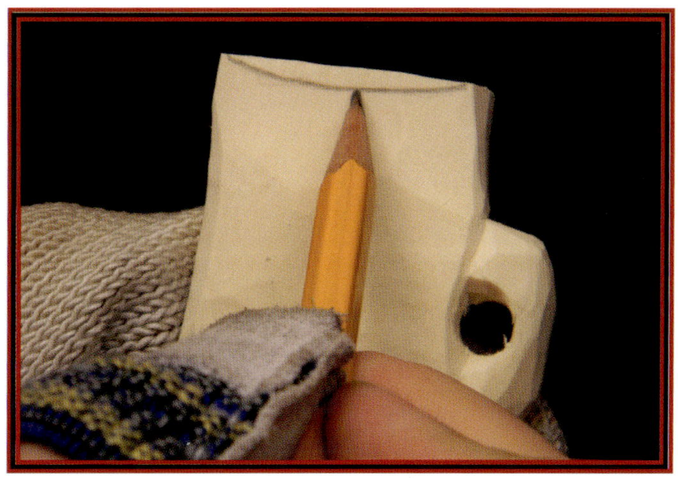

Now mark the rim of the mug… We will use the "V" tool to make this cut.

With the "V" tool, make the cut along the line marked ….

…. and then thin down the small area of wood.

Cut from the left side, removing a thin amount of wood. This gives the area a slightly beveled edge. The carving is now done.

I have marked the name in the middle of the mug and will use a wood-burner to burn the name and some accent lines on the outside of the mug.

Here are the name and accent lines burned.

Now place the pin back just above the center of the mug.

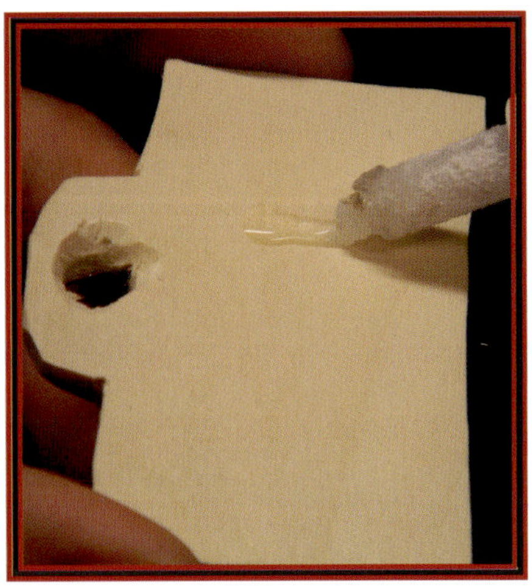

Add a bead of super glue to the area.

Press the pin back firmly in the bead of glue and let it dry.

Our coffee mug is complete and ready for its new owner.

4

I chose this pattern based on a smaller leaf that I had carved for my wife. It fit nicely into the standard size I tried to set for all the patterns in this book. Let the natural colors and shape of the leaf be your model as you carve this nametag.

# THE FALL LEAF

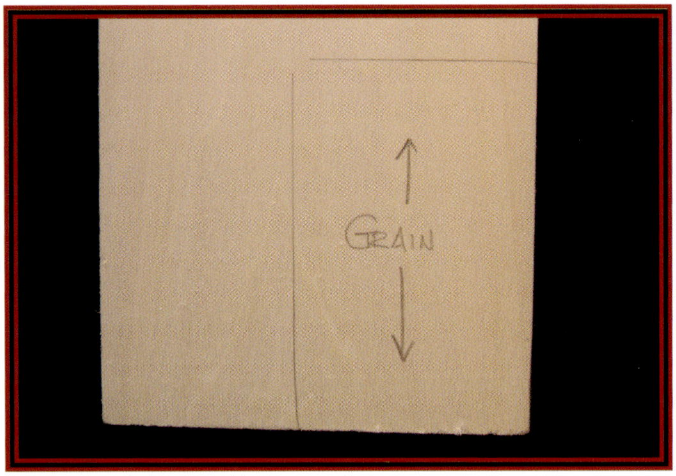


The leaf nametag grain will run from top to bottom.

Cut the block with a band saw and mark the leaf pattern.

Now we will cut along the lines to get our starting shape.

The edges are marked to start our first cuts: cleaning up the band saw marks.

I am making thin cuts to remove the marks and smooth the edges at the same time.

The grain changes a lot in this piece so cutting from both directions will be tricky and often. Take your time cutting in between the parts of the leaf.

Cut cross grain on the ends to avoid breaking the edges off.

We have the piece pretty clean at this point.

Mark the direction of your next cuts going with the grain. With these cuts, we will thin down the edges.

Make thin cuts at the end until you get close to the final thickness you want.

You can see the series of cuts I made to give me the shape I want.

Don't worry about rounding the inside of the leaf at this point…these cuts will be finished later.

With the top section cut, make the same cuts for the bottom section.

I am making thin scooping cuts along the edges of the leaf. I do this with a slight rolling motion of the knife blade as I cut up to give the leaf some shape.

We now have the face of the leaf carved, and it's starting to take shape.

Now we will move to cutting the edges of the leaf. When making these cuts, the depths of the cuts should vary so that they are not uniform.

Starting at the bottom, cut from the end towards the bottom and remove a small amount of wood. Work in the same area until you reach your stopping point.

This is the shape I wanted for the bottom. The more varying shapes and depths you have, the better the leaf will look.

Now cut down the other side of the bottom area making the same cuts as before.

The bottom of the leaf is done, showing the shape I wanted.

Round off the end here so that the piece does not look square. Continue working those cuts along the left side.

One half of the leaf complete. Repeat those same cuts to finish the other side.

Both sides are done.

Mark the inside points for your next cuts. For these cuts, we will use a #8 size palm gouge.

With the gouge, start at the bottom of the line marked and cut towards the inside point of the leaf.

Vary the depths of these cuts to make the leaf take shape.

One cut has been made.

Continue these cuts for all of the lines marked on the leaf, varying each cut depth.

This shows the leaf with the cuts finished. Next we will add more detail to the leaf.

Mark the areas in between the last cuts… We will use a #5 gouge to add texture.

Starting from the middle, cut towards the outside edge.

Make thin cuts each time until you reach a depth that looks good to you.

Texture has been added to one corner. Now continue working the area marked on the leaf.

After cutting the marked areas, make those cuts over the entire top of the leaf.

The finished side of the leaf.

Now to clean up the backside edges of the leaf, simply use the tip of the knife and round off the edge.

Clean up the back inside corners. Do this all the way around the carving.

On the backside of the leaf, make some scooping cuts so that the leaf will not look flat.

The cut should look like this... Repeat this for all the inside corners of the leaf.

Now mark the name and some accent lines... We will use a wood-burner to darken them.

Our finished carved leaf nametag.

Line up the pin back just above the middle and center of the leaf.

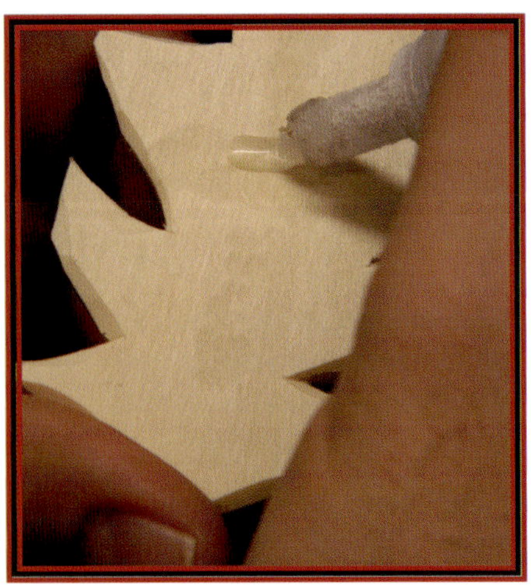

Apply a bead of super glue to the area.

Press the pin back firmly in the super glue and let it dry.

With the paint applied to the leaf, it is now finished.

5

This nametag is probably one of my favorites. I like the hillbilly styles of carvings that you see down here in the Ozarks. This was taken from a carving that I did for Helvie knives; although the idea has been around for a long time, I still thought it would make a great nametag for that special someone.

# THE OUTHOUSE

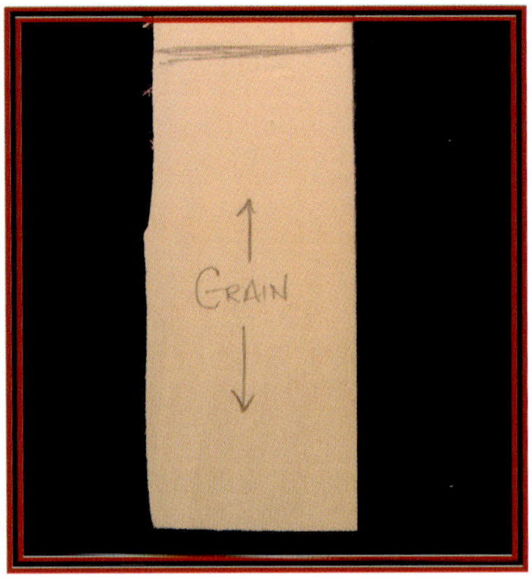


For the outhouse, I used a scrap piece of wood that is close to our rectangular pattern dimensions. The wood should have a thinner width and be taller with the grain running from top to bottom.

The pattern is marked. The areas we will be removing have an "x" on them. Cut the pattern with a band saw — the pattern shown has no pipe on the roof, but we will carve one on there.

The blank has been cut... I added the pipe coming out of the roof.

Now mark the sides of the carving to remove the band saw marks.

Start by making thin cuts along the edge. Pay close attention to the grain direction when cutting your edges: if you are feeling resistance in the wood, change the direction of your cuts.

Cut und... ...ve the band saw...

Cut towards the previous cut and clean up the inside corner. Continue cleaning up the edge around the entire block.

Now cut in... line marked.

...p cut along the line ... the left.

Continue the stop cut along the line.

With the knife ... make a thin cut up to the stop cut.

Repeat this thin cut along the bottom of the roof line.

This is what it should look like…we will thin it down a little later.

Now round the edges of the block.

Start about the mid-point of the block and cut towards the roof line, removing the edge of the block. Cut the edge off the entire length.

One side is done. Remove enough of the edge to take out its squared look.

Now let's remove the other side.

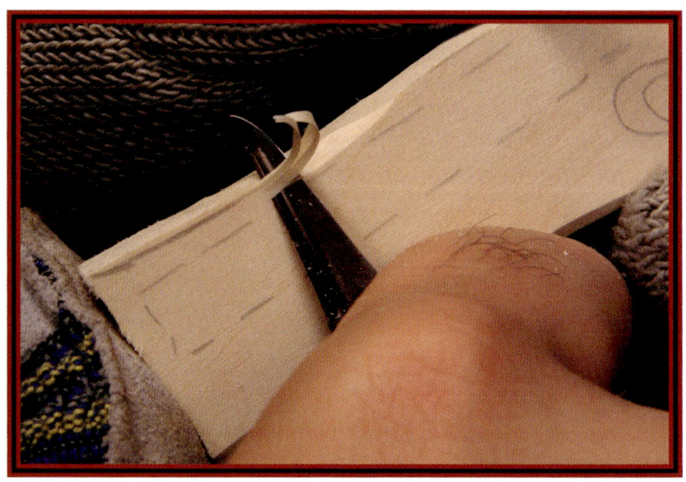

For this cut, I will start from the mid-point and cut down towards the bottom of the block.

Remove the face of the blank to give it a textured look.

Make a pare cut across the face of the block. These cuts do not need to be smooth and even.

Push cut towards the roof line, removing the wood.

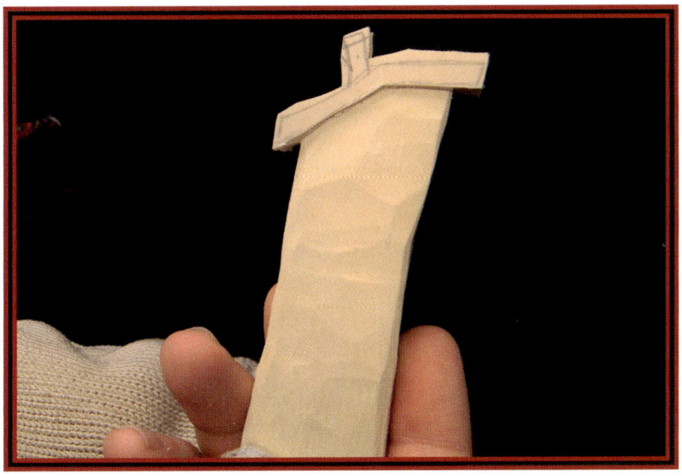

Now we have a surface ready for our pattern.

With the pattern back on the block, start cutting your trim lines. I used the "V" tool to make the next series of cuts.

Starting at the bottom, cut towards the roof line and define the trim of the outhouse.

We're almost finished cutting the trim on the right side.

Now make the same cut on the left side trim line.

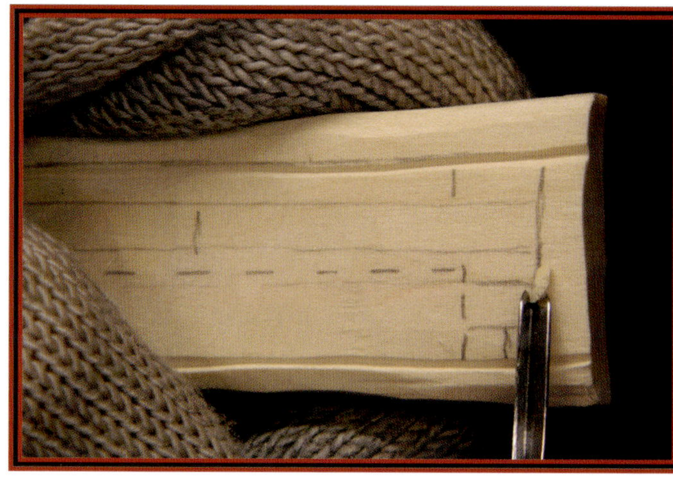

Cut across the blank on the bottom line. This cut is made with the "V" tool; we will be cutting across the grain.

Next, cut the board lines. These cuts will not be as deep as the trim lines.

Only a light pressure should be applied as these cuts are made. Cut all the vertical board lines marked. Make sure not to cut these lines where the name will be located.

The horizontal lines will be next.

Make light cuts with the "V" tool for these lines as well.

Now let's cut the area marked for the pipe.

Make a stop cut along the line marked.

Cut down towards the stop cut, removing the wood.

We will take off the wood a small amount at a time.

I have marked where I want my pipe thickness to stop. I will make the same thin cuts until I have removed this area.

Here is the thickness I was looking for on the pipe.

Now let's clean up the roof line.

Cutting from right to left, cut off the edge of the roof line.

Continue to clean up the edge of the roof.

The edge line is complete.

Mark the face of the roof line for the next cut.

With the blade fairly flat against the face, remove a thin layer of wood, cleaning it up.

Mark the shingle line as shown.

With the "V" tool, cut the lines marked.

This cut should be close to the same depth as the trim lines were.

Now mark the shingles of the roof.

These lines can vary in width to make the roof more interesting.

Cut the lines with the "V" tool.

With the tip of the knife, cut back towards the "V" cut to make the shingles look like they are stacked on top of each other.

This is what that cut looks like.

Continue with the cuts on each shingle along the roof.

Now round the two corners of the pipe and finish it.

The pipe corners are rounded and look good.

The carving is now done, and I wrote the name on the nametag.

With a wood-burner, I burned the name and accent lines on the outhouse. You can use a permanent marker for this process if you do not have a wood-burner.

Now line up the pin back on about center of the outhouse.

Apply a thin layer of super glue …

… and press the pin back firmly in place. Let it dry.

Our outhouse is completed with acrylic paints and it is now ready to be worn proudly.

# 6

The patterns that I have drawn for you to use are designed on the basis of two sizes. The round pattern is a 2-1/2" diameter circle and the rectangular pattern is 2-1/8" wide by 3-3/8" tall or the size of a standard credit card. These patterns can be enlarged or reduced to fit your specific needs, and are also universal. They can easily be changed into a sign or a wearable pin for the holidays. I tried to design patterns that were fun and not too complicated.

When I get asked to carve a nametag, I will draw out the pattern and color it just like you see it here in this chapter. This makes the final product easier to visualize and allows me to make color changes before the final color is applied.

I hope these patterns give you ideas to create that special nametag for friends and family members.

## PATTERNS

ONCE UPON...

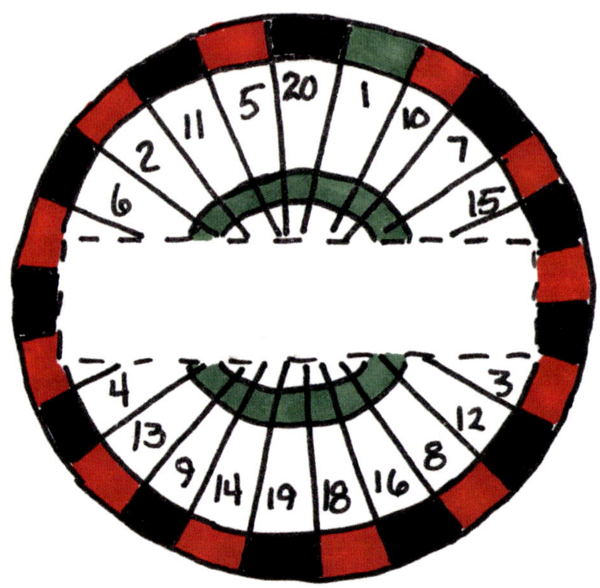
5 20 1 10 7 15
11 2 6
4 13 9 14 19 18 16 8 12 3

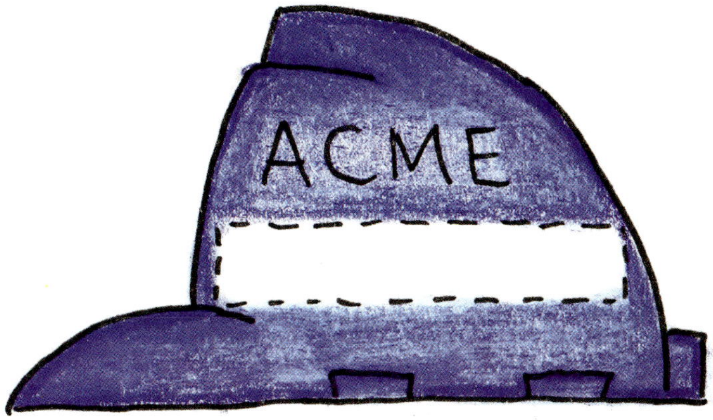
ACME

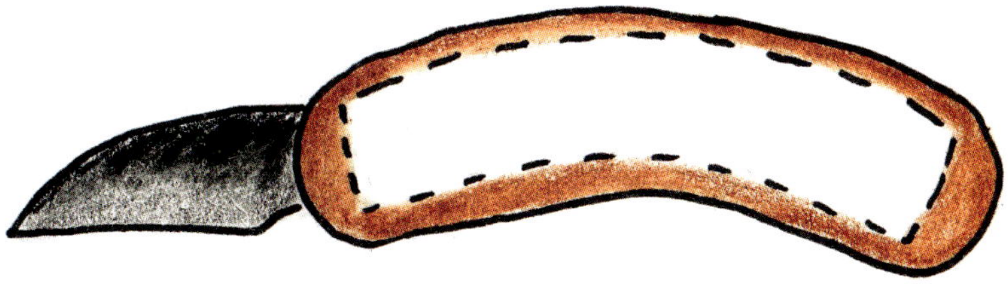

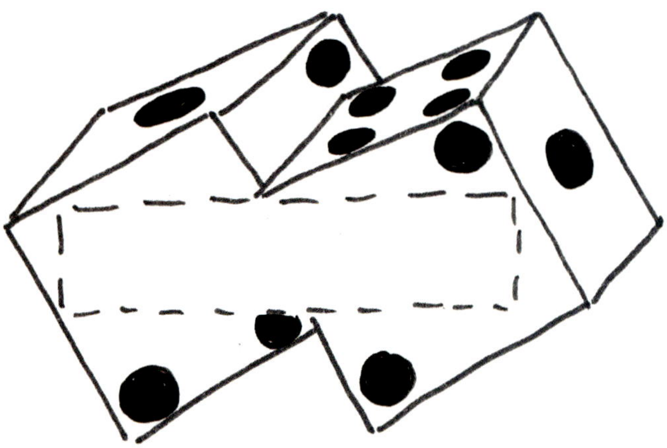

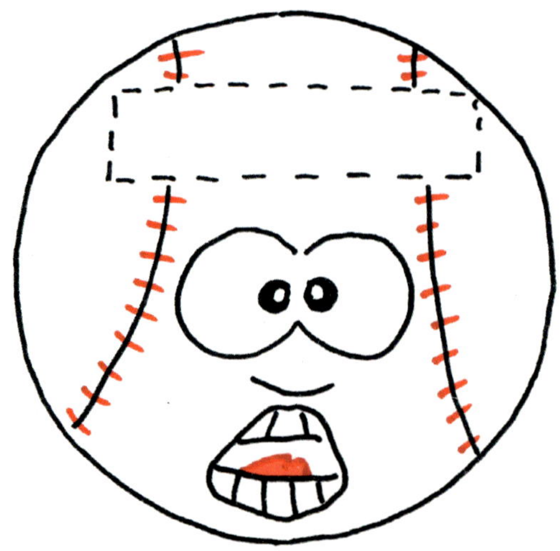

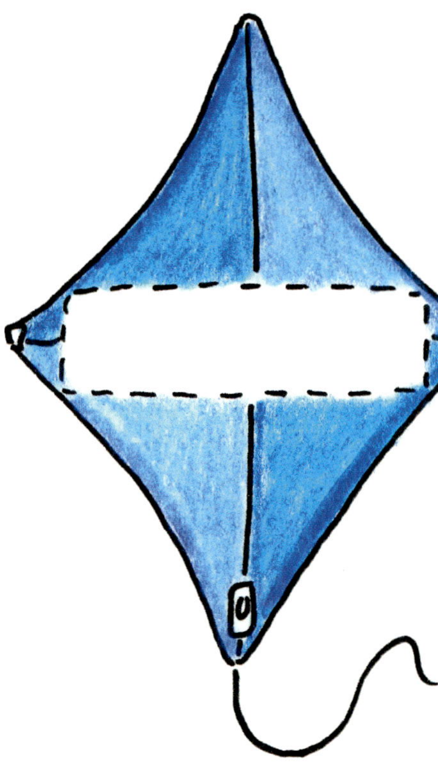